Fergus: Holiday Tales of a Scottish Terrier

A Country Life with Crazy Human Companions

As told to Sylvia R. Apple

Enjoy!

Sylvia R Apple

In memory of Ralph Webb
The Best Companion Ever

A Few Words of Introduction

The human mind fascinates me. As a
canine, I tend to remember the worst things that
happen to me, and not the good ones, because I
need to protect myself. Humans on the other
hand are quite opposite, they remember the
happy times, and tend to forget the bad times, or
they turn them into good times by a trick called
rationalizing. Happy holidays are often made up
of some not so happy events. Did the perfect
holiday dinner turn out to be a disaster because
the turkey was served almost raw? Did the warm
fire turn out to almost burn the house down? Did
the Christmas photo shoot end with the demise
of the Christmas tree? No matter how bad
separate events may be, humans remember the
total package with nostalgia, warmth, or at least
a sense of humor.

As a canine and companion of two rather eccentric humans (who asked me to refer to them as Mom and Dad, don't ask me why, they don't look anything like me), I have had the opportunity to witness the above mentioned and many more events. Most of these events took place in our Lone Pine Road home, out in the countryside of Central Pennsylvania. Other similarly ridiculous events have already been documented in my first book, Fergus: Memoirs of Scottish Terrier. I wanted to bring you a smaller book with stories that center on the holiday season. I didn't want it to be sentimental, though. We Scotties are not given to sentimentality. I took several stories from my memoirs to add to nine stories that have never been told before. I asked Mom (Sylvia) to interpret them into human language. I hope the words she generated by channeling me will help you all celebrate the fact that humans and canines share many experiences.

Thanksgiving—Fair and Fowl

As far as food and holidays go, nothing beats Thanksgiving in my opinion. It is my favorite holiday, and, on Lone Pine Road, usually a magnificent occasion. For as long as I can remember, our home has been the gathering place on Thanksgiving for the extended family and any new and/or international graduate students under Dad's guidance. Kids, dogs and grown-ups mix it up in syncopated chaos. For days ahead, Mom cooks up a storm, usually over-gauging the number of people she must feed by a few hundred. Therefore, I hang out in the kitchen. You never know when a dollop of food might slip to the floor. As chief taste tester, I try to stay alert and give Mom that "adorable dog" look. She is a real pushover for cuteness.

It helps that Mom is a taste tester, too. She usually has a very large bird cooking in the oven before breakfast. (She makes her stuffing the night before.) The aromas are intoxicating. It's almost more than I can endure, waiting eight to ten hours while smelling roast turkey. Mom also prepares carrots, onions, and potatoes and nests these beside the bird. The vegetables look like rare jewels set in a golden crown. (I would not have used this metaphor, but Mom insisted upon it. She is a poet of sorts.) When the bird is sizzling in its juices, she pulls pieces off to check if the bird is cooked. This is the best time to sit up, wag my tail, and stick out my tongue hopefully.

Mom lost her faith in meat thermometers, one fateful Thanksgiving, years ago, while Scott was still in college. She planned a huge meal for extended family that arrived with empty stomachs. As a growing teenager, Scott was especially hungry. Well, everything was in the oven and waiting for the turkey to roast. Mom kept checking the meat thermometer, which never budged from rare. Everyone tried to keep up the conversation and ignore the rumblings in their stomachs. Meanwhile the turkey was roasting away with all the trimmings on hold. Finally, Scott sat down on the floor, his back against the oven, in a hungry swoon. I guess he thought that he might hurry things along if he concentrated on the turkey. He was now beyond hungry. Mom moved her six-foot son out of the way of the oven door to check the thermometer again. It still had not reached the "done" line. She felt the day beginning to unravel. Friends and family looked stressed. Scott, his long legs spread out on the kitchen floor, was limp.

Desperate, Mom opened the oven and removed the bird. When she pulled at one of the turkey legs, it fell apart! The thermometer had failed. No need to get out the electric carving knife—this bird was completely filleted. Scott groaned, then leapt to his feet and devoured what seemed like half the turkey before Mom even had a chance to bring the bird to the table. There were no complaints however because everyone was just happy to chow down on the most tender turkey ever.

Another Thanksgiving for which Mom is famous (or should we say infamous) involved "The Great Corn Pudding Experiment." She loves to try out new and unusual recipes the way Dad loves to tinker with clocks and other gadgets. Every Thanksgiving she likes to put a dish on the table that does not fit the tradition of mashed potatoes, bread stuffing, corn, and cranberry sauce. Oh no. A meal comprised entirely of familiar dishes would be too simple. So Mom flips through the latest magazines looking for innovative twists on traditional holiday food. Normally, she does not have the time to try out any gems she discovers on Dad. Besides, she knows he will eat anything (except canned peas).

This particular Thanksgiving Mom had invited the minister, some graduate students from India, as well as family and Sarah, her adopted second mother. She decided to check out Yankee magazine for a truly early American Thanksgiving recipe. One caught her eye—Indian Corn Pudding. The recipe was said to be the original one given to New England settlers (if not to the Pilgrims themselves) by the Native Americans — who saw the newcomers starving because they did not know how to improvise. The Natives thought this situation ridiculous, and started giving the settlers cooking lessons, as Emeril gives his audiences on TV. (I sometimes watch cooking shows on TV, too.) America is an abundant continent. So what if the pigs run off or cows die? There were wild turkey, deer, and all kinds of small game for the Native Americans to hunt and trap. The Native Americans also showed the newcomers how to grow corn, tomatoes, and squash. Of course, the settlers showed their gratitude by stealing the Natives' land, but I digress.

The magazine depicted the corn pudding
served inside a plump pumpkin. Mom thought
the dessert looked very appealing, and decided to
try it out on Thanksgiving. The recipe called for
dried ground corn, molasses, and eggs. Mom
would need to bake the pudding for eight hours
in a slow oven, to mimic the settlers' preparation
in the fireplace cooking of old. She thought it
great that she could put the pudding into the
oven along with the turkey. Mom, you see, hates
to make pies. Pie is the only food that she has
failed to conquer. Her crusts turn out either
soggy or tough. Corn pudding seemed to be the
solution for a perfect, close to a traditional,
holiday dessert.

On Thanksgiving Day, everyone assembled
chatted gaily as Mom proudly put the food on
the table. The turkey came out perfectly juicy,
the stuffing perfectly browned. The mashed
potatoes were fluffy, and the vegetable casserole
smelled so good, even to the children. Everyone

agreed this was a "real" Thanksgiving. Then for dessert, Mom brought to the table a huge pumpkin filled with Indian Corn Pudding.

"Where's the pumpkin pie?" one child asked.

"And the whipped cream?" asked another.

"The Pilgrims didn't have pumpkin pie or whipped cream," Mom replied. "We're going to have the traditional dish served on the first Thanksgiving."

Obviously, Mom served the dish with good intentions, but it turned out to be a fiasco. The graduate students gulped down the pudding with pained smiles. The other adults began to slide away from the table. The kids literally ran from the dessert, unashamed to declare it "YUCKY." Only the minister and his wife finished their portions. The minister's wife actually ate a second helping, but declined to take the leftover pudding home. In fact, she looked a little green around the gills and went home early. Later, someone snuck out to the Mini Mart and brought back ice cream. This person was received as a hero.

Mom pouted for a while, but soon found the "Corn Pudding Experiment" as amusing as everyone else did. "You would have starved as pilgrims!" she laughed.

She ate as much of the pudding as she could herself, but ended up throwing the bulk of it away. Thank heavens I was not there (not having been born yet) to receive *those* leftovers!

Now there are two foods Dad will not eat—canned peas and corn pudding.

Let It Snow

There are years in Halfmoon Valley
when it hardly snows at all and years when it
never stops snowing. Mom says that there is
something called La Nina (which means "little
girl"), way out in the Pacific Ocean a gazillion
miles away, that causes our weather to change
and become dryer and warmer than usual. Then
in some years there is El Nino (which means
"little boy"), that causes the opposite. (The idea
that a little boy or a little girl way out in the
Pacific Ocean could cause such wild swings in
our weather in Halfmoon Valley is hard to
believe.) Whatever the cause, we canines are
very sensitive to the changes. On the one hand
our noses enjoy all the scents of the earth when
there is no snow. Now that doesn't mean we
can't sniff out a rabbit hole through snow cover,
we canines can smell a rabbit a mile away. But
without snow cover our nasal radar is more

enhanced. On the other hand, it's easier to pick up the tracks of furry critters when there is snow on the ground.

Whether the weather is wet or dry, snowy or just damp, Lone Pine Road, the gravely road in front of our property, is the artery by which all the human creatures living adjacent must move about. And this road is close to my heart. I don't say this because I am sentimental. We Scots are practical if nothing else. No, I say this because, as a Scottie, I am built very low to the ground and have a "kilt" on my underside, which means I literally come in contact with Lone Pine Road when I traverse its gritty surface. So I am very well acquainted with its idiosyncrasies.

Lone Pine Road began as a farm lane, built up with layers of ash and gravel. It is named for a giant pine tree that sits majestically at the end of this quarter mile thoroughfare. Our house slumbers on its boundary at the far end, but we own a slice of the road running along this boundary. (That makes Mom and Dad responsible partially for its upkeep, more about this later). Bed rock is a long way down, so I always sense the shifts and rumbles of the earth as if we were residing on the caldera of a sleeping volcano. You see Lone Pine is no ordinary immutable road. It is not built of rock, concrete and/or macadam (invented by another practical Scotsman). Oh no, Lone Pine Road actually has a life of its own. It is built over a strange geological mixture of soft, pitted limestone covered with sandy marsh soil and topped off with fly ash (a powdery substance left from mining operations in the 19th century) and a sprinkling of gravel. The fly ash is sticky when wet and sooty when dry. Either way I come home with a good deal of it clinging to my fur. When it snows I become the "abominable snowdog."

The road is also soggy most of the time because it sits at the lowest point in the valley on the edge of a huge pine barren, which acts as a sponge for the entire watershed. This is where most of the runoff water in the region eventually finds its way. Sinkholes abound in this region. These sinkholes erupt when a spontaneous collapse of the water soaked limestone below forms yawning gaps in the earth. Some are big enough to accommodate old refrigerators, tractor tires, soccer balls, car parts, and heaven knows what else. Of course they are great hiding places for groundhogs, too. There are a number of these sinkholes along the road, so every outing, amble, or drive is fraught with adventure for humans as well as other animals.

I travel Lone Pine Road everyday with Mom for our trips to the mailbox – at the other end of the lane – then we hike on out into the fields and woodlands which fan out from there. It's all up hill in any direction from this end of our gritty shifting, ash laden lane. But Mom and I like the exercise, and the adventures which await us. It's when we return home that I must face a nasty brushing and shake down as I deposit a goodly amount of the road and surroundings on to the tile floor inside the door. Whether its snow, sand, ash or small gravel, it all collects on my kilt, the long fur extending from my belly. I have a kilt because it protects me, as I've explained in my memoirs, but it also puts me in direct contact with the road. This explains my intimate knowledge of the road and perhaps my preoccupation with it, too.

The humans living along Lone Pine Road are much more removed from the particles that make up the road than I am. So they don't think about it much except when they either get stuck in its waterlogged ruts or slide off an unforgiving ice patch. However, it is snow that brings humans and other creatures the most excitement along this road – snow in amounts not recorded at the weather station, snow that tumbles out of the sky with torpedo precision and hurricaneintensity, snow that gets compacted and turns to ice, the kind of snow that turns into legend.

Our snow storms isolate us from the rest of the world, because we are not connected to any governmental system here. Halfmoon Township won't send a snow plow. The county doesn't seem to know we exist, and the road doesn't even appear on any official state map. Basically we're left to fend for ourselves. Now these circumstances might worry most people, but not the diehards who live here. These humans shun governmental assistance. And, don't tell anyone, but there are a few who may actually be hiding out from the law. So when it comes to snow, Lone Pine residents are left to their own devices. Each household owns a strip of road in front of their property. This makes for a kind of anarchy. There is a neighborhood association, but no one comes to the infrequent meetings. No one pays dues for the gravel, and no one follows the rules. Dad tried going door to door to collect enough money for a load of gravel and had more than one door slammed in his face.

This is how people manage the road when snow is forecast, they divide and conquer. The strip closest to Sawmill Road, our only exit, is owned by the telephone company, which has a tiny switching station on the corner. We know that the first 50 feet of our road will be quickly cleared. Next along the road are the Meyers. They are responsible for the next 100 feet or so. They are diligent but lack the heavy equipment to plow the entire road. So we'll take a look at the folks who live at the other end of the road. Brook (and his wife) lives at the far end next to us, and this guy has more recreational vehicles than many used car lots. He has collected everything from a reclining bicycle to a heavy duty pick-up with a snow plow attached. Without any regulation or formal agreement, we all know he will be pushing a path through the snow to the other end of the road before dawn – that is if the snowfall stops at 12 inches or so, which is what his plow can handle. To hear him rev up his truck in the wee small hours is to know we may get to the mailbox or the grocery store before spring thaw.

There are times, though, when others along the road have created havoc, especially when we get more than 12 inches of snow overnight. Most humans living along the road have 4-wheel drive vehicles. Some of these humans pull out on the road at full tilt using these vehicles like battering rams, creating so many ruts in the snow or ash that the rest of population can't maneuver. These are the renegades. It makes them happy to leave the rest of the little community in the dust – or snow as the case may be. It isn't unheard of for four or five SUVs to try breaking the world's record for number of feet of snow a 4-wheel drive can tunnel through. Instead they get stuck in the white stuff. Often a sort of train wreck occurs. It isn't uncommon, after a snowstorm of 12 inches or more, for four or five SUVs to pile up and create an impasse without them ever actually touching each other. Instead they each have a huge snow pile in front of them. If you have ever seen a train stuck in the snow (like the Orient Express), you will get the picture. You can see why I love to wake up early after a big storm and hear a chain reaction of soft thuds out on Lone Pine Road. I know the day will be filled with excitement, as the world of humans and their machines comes to a halt.

Each driver jumps out of his or her vehicle and begins to shout at all the others lined up in this chain reaction of stupidity. Civility, a quality in short supply under normal circumstances, is completely missing from these interactions. Mom is wise to stay put on these occasions, but we can usually hear the swear words from one end of the road to the other.

There was one particular day when I watched as Brook attempted to plow out the driveway to our house. The snow was coming down so unrelentingly that his truck was overwhelmed and buried up to the fenders within minutes. It looked as if a dump truck in the sky chose to empty its entire load of snow on Brook's truck. His wheels spun. He put the gear in reverse and then in forward a number of times, but to no avail (that means no luck. My interpreter likes to use old English). When the snow is this deep there's only one man with the equipment to handle the situation – that's Allen. Allen moved into our neighborhood a few months before this historic event. He owns an excavating business and has machinery that is bigger than the three-bay garage he bought along with the Slear's house. Mom was alarmed when she first saw this machinery roll down the lane next to our house. She pictured bivouacs with AK 47s and men in camouflage descending on the gentle folks out here in Halfmoon Valley.

Well her fears were unfounded. Allen digs holes, big holes, hauls gravel and can fill a sinkhole with ease. In fact, he turned out to be the neighborhood hero. He pulled Brook out of the driveway after the blizzard that day and scooped out the snow surrounding the stranded SUVs that blocked the road. He even filled a sinkhole that Mom almost drove into with the riding mower back in our woods one summer, but that's another story. So, when a blizzard is forecast or a huge tree falls across the road, or the ruts get so deep I can't see over them, the good people of Lone Pine Road knock on his door.

Mom and I have braved all kinds of weather to reach the mailbox, but it is the most fun when we can watch Allen on his Bobcat scooping up and dumping enough snow off the road to build a military size fort (not for hostile occupation, but to open an exit to the wider world) so the stranded citizens on Lone Pine Road, a country road unknown to the rest of the world, can go about their lives.

Walking on Thin Ice

Mom and I often have to travel Lone Pine Road when the ice has formed on the surface like a skating rink. Neither of us is ever prepared for this. We careen along the ruts as if we were both as drunk as skunks. Now this might be humorous to Mom, but it is demoralizing to me. I hunt skunks. I don't like to look undignified. Scotties are a dignified bred. To help me feel better Mom remembered her first Christmas married to Dad and unraveled the tale for me. This is my version of it.

Mom and Dad's first home together was a 1920's bungalow in a, mostly safe, university town with little crime beyond student "up risings" and petty theft. Their porch furniture was chained in place, though, and the noise level on the weekends could be described as a herd of wild cats on the prowl. This was Dad's house when he met Mom who had always dreamed of

Christmas in an old house with a stone fireplace and heavy oak columns. The catch was that the old house needed a lot of restoration. With so much restoration work going on, Mom was not in a hurry to move in. She waited until Dad had repaired, recycled and restored the house before she accepted his proposal and finally tied the knot.

Needless to say they had a long engagement. Dad even replaced a gigantic oil burning furnace with a new gas burning model – all by himself. This took months. (I guess Mom wanted to make sure it wouldn't blow up before she took up residence.) Sometimes Mom would visit Dad and urge him to take a break from furnace building to get some fresh air. The basement was one of those that truly fit the description of a basement – dark, damp and full of cob webs. But Dad seemed to thrive in places like this – so much so that Mom accused him of being a vampire. In this case I can empathize with Dad. I think he may have invented the phrase "man cave." I wasn't around at the time, but I would have appreciated the atmosphere. My ancestors the wolves have used caves as dens for eons.

Mom wasn't idle during this house renovation time either. As Dad was working on his "bachelor project," Mom was actually building new home for her two kids, Scott and Amy, and herself. She found a contractor and, after a year of filling out forms, she had a mortgage guaranteed by the U. S. government. Now her dream of being a home owner was coming true. The only problem was that, in order to stay within her budget, most of the inside finishing work on the new house was allocated to her and her family. There were hundreds of board feet of molding to sand, stain and varnish. The kids were not thrilled, and the work went on for almost a year. Wedding plans were put on hold. Mom had so much invested in the house, she wanted to live in it a while.

It amazes me how much trouble humans go to in order to have a place to eat and sleep. First they have to go to a job every day, often doing something they don't like, in order to earn money. You can't eat money or sleep on it, though some humans stick it under their mattresses. Oh no. You have to use money to buy food and houses. That's because all the land for growing food and forests where the game lives gets farther and farther way. It's being taken over by – you guessed it – housing developments.

Ah well, back to the story of Mom and Dad's first Christmas together. (They did eventually marry, opting to rent out the new house and live in the old one.) Mom was planning a festive Christmas with family. She pictured a lovely fresh evergreen tree in the niche by the stone fireplace. Dad had different

29

ideas. He was used to digging one out of the dumpsters on campus after Penn State closed for the holidays. Yep, he was a dumpster diver. He talked Mom into at least inspecting the possibilities before turning up her nose. She gave in, and they brought home a tree that seemed fine at the time. (It was only leaning against the dumpster, not in it.) However, before they could get the lights on it, it began to shed its needles. Mom used hairspray in the hopes of retaining at least half the needles. They had to place the ornaments strategically to hide the bare spots. It goes without saying that this was the one and only time Mom would allow a tree from a dumpster to come into her home.

On the morning of Christmas Eve, a light rain began to fall. Mom had no idea that an ice storm was in the making. Scott and Amy were there on break from med school and nursing school, respectively. Breakfast was on the stove.

Mom was unaware that a thin layer of dangerous ice was forming outside.

The bungalow sits atop a steep incline. Sixteen concrete steps lead up from the street below. Mom usually let Dad get the morning paper. But she didn't want to wake him. It would have turned out better if she had awakened him. Dad knew the steps well and had once managed to successfully careen down all sixteen steps during an ice storm and land in the middle of the street on his feet without a blemish. It helps to be agile in a situation like this. Dad is very agile and very lucky, having escaped a number of disastrous events. In fact, to say Dad is lucky is an understatement. He is a major survivor. This man has tempted fate enough times to make the nine lives of a cat seem paltry. Like the energizer bunny, he just keeps going and going.

People love to hear the stories of Dad's near death experiences. There is one year that stands out in terms of survival for Dad. It was 1948. He was14 years old, and exploring the world in interesting ways. He took risks and ended up almost getting killed several times. The most serious event was not of his making, though. It occurred at the local drive-in theater where Dad earned money cleaning windshields so people could see the movie screen better. Another kid his age, Clark, who worked there as a projectionist, was one of those unruly teenagers Dad knew. But unlike Ralph (Dad), this kid had guns and would shoot at jack rabbits from his jeep as he drove at breakneck speed over the prairie. One night he aimed his pistol at Dad and pulled the tiger. No one ever found out exactly why. (If I had been there, I would have torn that kid apart.)

Dad said simply, "You got me Clark. Take me to the hospital." He barely realized what had happened to him before he keeled over.

The owner of the drive-in heard the gun go off and had Dad in his car racing for the hospital within minutes. Dad's mother and grandmother had been watching the movie, and were following behind. The quick action of the drive-in owner and the fact that a surgeon fresh from the battle fields of WWII was there to operate immediately, doubtless saved Dad's life. He could have bled to death. The bullet split his vena cava in two and shot off his appendix. It went through his intestines and logged in his pelvis. It's still there today. Two hundred and sixty-three penicillin shots were needed to keep peritonitis from taking his life after the surgery. Amazingly, it never occurred to Dad that his life might be in danger.

Now that we've established Dad's survival skills, let's just say Mom is not as agile or lucky. To say she's ungraceful on her feet would be unkind but accurate. She spontaneously decided to go out and get the paper while her two children ate breakfast. The ice waiting for her was black ice – the kind you can't see. She swung the door open and took one fateful step off the porch. She went up in the air and came down on her back. As she lay there her mind was still reaching for the paper. It took a few seconds for her brain to register where she was. She must have screamed, but didn't feel the pain until Scott, the med student, and Amy the nurse arrived to help. The moment they tried to get her upright, the pain took over.

Hearing Scott say, "Call an ambulance!" is all she recalls. After that she blanked out. She was literally going into shock, so she missed the discussion about who would accompany her to the hospital. Scott won out. The ambulance volunteers put her on a stretcher with wheels and covered her with her coat, putting the hood of the coat over her face, since icy rain continued to fall. It so happened that the next door neighbor saw the stretcher with a fully shrouded human

form being wheeled away from the back of the
house (where there were only two steps) and
came to an unsettling conclusion. They thought
she must be dead. However, Mom's demise was
greatly exaggerated, as Mark Twain would say.
Mom was just greatly inconvenienced. She
ended up in a supply closet at the hospital,
because the emergency room was packed to the
gills with other unlucky black ice victims.

While Scott searched for a doctor, the
family searched for her. The door to the closet
had been bumped closed by mistake, and Mom
couldn't move to open it. Finally a volunteer
who knew Mom happened to go for supplies and
saw her on the stretcher shaking from the cold
and recovering from shock. He tucked a blanket
around her and wheeled her up to the x-ray
room. A few hours later, she was told she had a
badly bruised sciatic nerve. Pain meds and a
back brace made it possible for her to get into a
car to come home. The neighbor who had feared

the worst was astonished to see Mom gingerly being helped down the walk to the back door.

Christmas was not quite the festive occasion Mom had envisioned. But, despite her pain, she felt lucky. Her two children were with her. Others made the Christmas dinner, set the table and wrapped the gifts. She was ensconced in a reclining chair, which would serve as her (not final) resting place 24 hours a day for three weeks. (She could pull a lever on the side to be gently ejected upright so she could go to the bathroom.) Much of the holiday was spent in a happy haze, induced by pain medication. And she felt her kids had gotten some good first hand experience for their future professions. As for Dad, he was very solicitous. He decided to tear out a number of the concrete steps and terrace the hillside, as soon as the snow melted -- which he did all by himself. It seems the restoration on the bungalow was not quite over.

"So you see," said Mom as we slipped and skidded our way to the mailbox on Lone Pine Road, " I'm just happy we have no steps to maneuver each time we leave the house."

I had to agree with that. I would look even less dignified careening down icy steps on a busy street. And there would be no skunks to hunt. All this made our home out on this country road seem like the ideal place for our family. And it was!

The Christmas Photo Shoot

One year, long before there was even snow on the ground, Dad had a plan for Christmas time. Of course this involved one of his new gadgets. It was not a very big gadget, but it made me nervous. It looked like a gigantic spider or a long thin stand for a gun. Either possibility was unpleasant. When Dad aimed it in my direction, I got the distinct feeling that I was a target. It didn't look like a regular gun, and it only made a clicking sound when he pressed the trigger. Even so, I took off whenever I saw Dad setting it up.

You see, Mom has sensitized me to guns, saying all guns are dangerous whatever the size. We often see hunters carrying guns into the woodland nearby. The game lands are so close to Lone Pine Road that these guys often enter our property in search of game, in spite of the notices that tell them to stay away. They have one thing on their collective minds – to kill an animal, any animal. You could see it in their eyes if you wished to risk getting close enough. Starting on October first each year, Mom makes me wear a ridiculous orange "vest" whenever we go out. The kids in the neighborhood (some of whom actually have guns themselves) laugh and ask if I'm dressing as a pumpkin for Halloween. So, just stepping outside the door can be dangerous, or at least embarrassing.

Guns start going off at dawn on the first day of hunting season and continue to fire for months. First there's small game season, then turkey, then bear, then deer season. There's even a season for muskets and one for bow and arrows. I wouldn't be surprised if there is one for AK47's. In fact there are enough hunters in Pennsylvania alone to make up a standing army to match that of North Korea. And you'd think a major military skirmish had just begun on that first day of hunting season. POP! BANG!

KABOOM! The woods are crawling with "mutant ninjas" with hands attached to gleaming metal barrels – their brains squeezed to a point just behind the guns' sites. Some of the guns are as big as the humanoids behind them. Mom calls the creatures that come too close to our home *poachers* with the kind on distain she usually reserves for most politicians. I think they have some human characteristics, because they shout words at each other. But most of these words would not be allowed in our house. They are the four letter kind, as Mom would say.

But I digress. Dad's only rifle sits in a closet behind the clothes, wrapped in a blanket. The instrument he was pointing at me couldn't be a gun. It had three legs like a spider on steroids, and I may have seen Mom using the device when she hangs her quilts on the wall for photographing. She spends a lot of time clicking away, and, so far, there are no powder burns or holes in her quilts. So I surmised that it was a camera Dad had been aiming at me, but why?

Suddenly I was remembering an incident from my distant past. I was still living with my former family and we were visiting Mom and Dad at their former house in the city. Arleigh, the little girl in our family, was only a year old at the time. Scott and Dot, Arleigh's mom and dad, were setting up a camera in front of the fireplace to take pictures of their family for Christmas cards.

This was my first Christmas, too. I had no idea what to expect but there seemed to be a great deal of activity surrounding this event. Arleigh was dressed in a strange costume of petticoats, ruffles and bows. It was hard to see her little body amidst all the clothing. I was just glad it wasn't me who had to wear this outfit. The family all appeared to be dressed in what I later learned was holiday attire.

They practiced arranging themselves around the stone fireplace and smiling at the funny instrument with the three legs sitting in front of them. Dad had placed a tray with hot tea and cookies on the coffee table to enjoy after this event. As all this was taking place the grown-ups lost track of Arleigh who had wondered over to the tray of goodies. The leaf on the coffee table gave way as Arleigh crawled on it to retrieve a cookie. With a loud bang, the toddler, the tray, the cookies and the hot tea all came crashing to the floor. It only took seconds for her dad to scoop her up and run into the kitchen, just as she screamed from the burn of the tea. She was plunged under the sink filled with running cold water, tights, ruffles, bows and all. Now this to her was adding insult in injury. First she thought she was punished with hot tea, then freezing cold water just because she wanted a cookie!

When everything settled down and it was clear she was only a little red from the tea, the photo shoot continued. But the little girl in the resulting photos still had a trembling chin and a tear sliding down her cheek. I was able to stay out of harms way, but the incident left an indelible mark on my psyche.

While I was remembering this event, Mom came in and explained that Dad was preparing for a Christmas photo of the three of us, and needed a tripod (the three legged thing) to steady the camera so he could use a timer to get us all in the picture. But first we had to set up the Christmas tree and decorate it. Since we would be leaving it up until Christmas, more than a month away, it had to be an artificial tree. I always loved when a real evergreen was brought into the house. The woodsy odor awoke images of the dens of my ancestors the wolves. This new tree was not the same.

To start with, Mom and Dad had a terrible time putting it together. It came in a big box, totally dismembered. All the "branches" looked the same except for their size. Dad would put a branch into the center pole, only to be admonished by Mom for inserting a bottom branch into the middle layer. She didn't seem to have any better luck herself, so she quietly went to look for the decorations. The "tree" began to look awfully lopsided. It tilted like Dad's sailboat mast in a stiff wind. Soon it fell over. "D---," said Dad. He picked it up and studied the configuration. All the branches came back off. He measured and numbered each branch. After that he was ready to rebuild the tree. After hours of assembly, it still tilted precariously.

"It has a natural look," he said as he inserted the crowning sprig. Mom only groaned when she saw it. She was so reluctant to give up the idea of having in a lovely spruce or Douglas fir, she almost wept. But Dad had convinced her that this was a more environmentally friendly solution.

"I guess when it's decorated, it will be better," she sighed. She got out her box of mostly handmade ornaments, created from things like milkweed pods and teasels tied with ribbons. And for the top of the tree – she began unwrapping a cornhusk angel. The only problem was that Dad was still trying to get their ancient string of lights to work. He had assembled his volt meter, electrical tape, extra bulbs and a tangled mass of wires. Getting this tree adorned was going to be a lengthy process at best.

I lay down in my bed for a nap. Humans can sometimes exhaust a dog. We canines know how to focus on the important things in life – food, water, food, walks, food and sleep. Humans seem to have an over abundance of food. Actually they have an over abundance of everything. Their possessions pile up and take all kinds of space and time to maintain, so much so that humans lose their focus. Dad does not like to discard anything, though, and he loves a challenge. So he tries each year to get the Christmas lights all blinking at once. Mom could easily hop in the car, drive ten miles to Walmart, buy new lights and drive back, with a stop for coffee, before Dad would have the old ones working. However, Mom knows that Dad would just wave her off and continue with his quest, then return the new lights to the store. So she goes to her studio to paint instead of going to Walmart. At least they got a head start on the tree this year. It could end up taking a month to assemble.

Finally Dad got all the lights working and on the tree. Mom hung the ornaments. It didn't look too bad, if you tilted your head when you looked at the tree. It wasn't any tree my ancestors would have chosen to nest under, but then Mom wouldn't want a pack of wolves hanging out in her living room anyway.

The time had arrived for the "photo shoot" as Dad ominously called it. I had been hearing distant gun shots from some rogue hunters' guns all day, and I was a little nervous about anything to do with shooting. Dad set up his spider legged contraption. Mom changed into a colorful outfit. They arranged some seats in front of the Christmas tree and coaxed me out of my bed. I didn't want to be in the photo shoot, having a sense of déjà vu about the incident with Arleigh and fearing that a gun might be involved after all. Dad set a timer on the camera that ticked like a time bomb. He quickly knelt beside Mom, while she held on to my collar. The camera flashed and I jumped.

"Darn," said Dad. "We have to try again."

The next time he didn't get into place before the flash went off, and the camera only got Mom and me. By this time Mom was chuckling at the whole affair. On the third try Mom and Dad were in place, but I was definitely ducking. On the fourth try Dad had a grip on me, but Mom was laughing, because I was trying to squirm out of his grasp.

Suddenly a real gun went off not far from the house. Kaboom! I bolted backward and knocked into the tree. It came crashing down on top of Mom and Dad. Lights flickered, and popped, causing the sparks. Ornaments sprung from their perches, and artificial branches flipped off the "trunk." At first Mom and Dad seemed stunned. No one was hurt, but the photo shoot was definitely over. Dad was really upset because his tripod and camera went over with the tree. Mom was so angry with the hunter who shot off his gun so close to our house that she tramped out on the deck and gave him a piece of her mind while plucking artificial pine needles and cornhusk ornaments out of her hair. The hunter must have thought Mom was another hunter in camouflage. I was under the coffee table trailing ribbon and tree lights. I don't know if I was more afraid of the hunter or Dad. I had ruined his plan to have early Christmas pictures for cards. I came out from under the table when he offered me a biscuit. He was just glad I wasn't hurt.

Mom and Dad decided not to put the tree up again that year. Getting it done once was trouble enough. Anyway Mom insisted on new lights for the next year, and Dad agreed thinking he had converted her to a fake tree. To my complete relief there was never another Christmas photo shoot. The photos that resulted from this fiasco were so ridiculous they became the hit of family gatherings that year.

Bunny Business

As the holiday season approaches, Lone
Pine Road is fraught with activity – at least for
the humans living there. The whole community
seems to be connected by one long string of
blinking lights. Out here in the country you
don't see elegant Martha Steward (Who is she
anyway?) displays of tiny white lights perfectly
laced onto the branches of perfectly shaped
spruce trees. On no – what you see along our
road is mismatched strings of colored bulbs
draped across fence posts and tractors, dangling
from old trees and even outlining half collapsed
shed roofs.

Somehow this haphazard collection of
holiday decorations (including three plastic
blowup snowmen) seems happier than those of
Martha's urban disciples. The fact that hard
working people take the time to decorate at all
shows their deep connection to the season.

The farmers, plumbers, construction workers and delivery men put on a show that they know few will see except those of us living here. At the far end of the road lives a family that hardly speaks to anyone else. Their life has been saddened by the death of a child, but they put up so many lights at Christmas time, the usually visible stars are dimmed by the glow.

It's so cloudy here in Halfmoon Valley that the lights stay on and can be seen all day – sometimes helping Mom and I find our way on the rutted road through dense fog. We usually have lots of snow this time of year, of course, which actually adds several amps of daylight wattage. Many days the earth is brighter than the sky, or at least it looks that way. As a Scottie, I love the weather here. This is the kind of weather my ancestors "enjoyed" back in Scotland. Mom has told me stories of her year in Scotland – traipsing across the country in search of Celtic carved stones. She described the ever changing climate, which, on one particular day started out at 72 degrees in Dunkeld and ended in a snow storm near Aberdeen. Of course, she had traveled in her little car 40 miles into the Cairngorm Mountains before the snow hit. This was in May!

The car had a faulty heater, so she needed a drastic change of wardrobe which she didn't have. She arrived at the bed and breakfast, where she had reserved a room, in a spasm of shivers. The lady who owned the B and B (a private home in a small village) took one look at Mom and wrapped her in a down comforter. She put Mom to bed with a hot water bottle and brought up hot tea and fresh, warm scones. As Mom began to thaw out, she realized she was being treated like a long lost relative instead of a perfect stranger. Her gratitude was immense.

I wish I could have traveled through Scotland with Mom, but I wasn't born yet. However, Mom says that the weather in

Halfmoon Valley is a lot like the high valleys of Scotland, so much so that I wouldn't know the difference. Besides there are more critters here to keep me occupied. This weather is just suited to a husky breed like mine, especially in the winter. You see Scottish terriers actually have two coats of fur most of the year. The undercoat is like humans' long underwear. It keeps us warm even in blizzard conditions.

We don't have many blizzards in Halfmoon Valley because it is surrounded on three sides by mountains which protect us. But once in a while frigid gale force winds sweep in and give us a "white out." We all have to hunker down then – animals and humans alike. On Lone Pine Road we are lucky to have a barrier of tall pine and oak trees along the north side of the road. Even so Mom and I sometimes get caught in a bad squall out in the fields or returning from the mail box. December, even before the official start of winter, is often the coldest time of year here. The Christmas decorations can end up blowing into a neighbor's yard. I once saw a half deflated snowman up in a tree waving as if he wanted to be rescued.

I get excited with the first snow, which is usually before Christmas. This excitement is passed on to Mom who describes herself as a "snow bunny." This isn't an image I like to contemplate – Mom with big ears and a fluffy tail. But she and Dad have a thing about bunnies. He calls her "Bunny" and she buys him bunny objects. We have bunny salt and pepper shakers, bunny napkin rings, a bunny bread board, and bunny candle holders, etc, etc.

Mom and Dad do look kind of ridiculous once they're dressed to go out. But their appearance is more like yaks than bunnies. It seems to me that getting ready to face the cold takes humans an inordinate amount of time. All I need is my collar and leash, but Mom suits up in so many layers you can only recognize her by her scent.

Dad actually has a real rabbit fur hat with ear flaps and a chin strap. It's a wonder some wayward hunter hasn't blown Dad's head off. Humans wearing any kind of animal fur give me the creeps. The outfit Dad usually puts on to clear the driveway includes this furry monstrosity of a hat, as well as a purple down jacket and hunting boots. To say he looks a little like the cartoon character, Elmer Fudd, is an understatement.

Dad loves any excuse to start up a machine, so he rubs his hands together and heads for the shed to get the snow blower whenever the first flakes fall. He hasn't quite mastered the directional nozzle on the blower, though, so by the time he has scooped up most of the snow in the drive way, he is wearing a goodly amount of it himself. He's covered in the white powdery stuff from bunny hat to hunting boot. When he's finished Mom says he looks like the "Abominable Bunny". Needless to say, Mom and I have learned to stay indoors when this operation is taking place.

At holiday time Mom and I go out in the snow with very different goals in mind. Mom is focused on collecting winter berries, evergreen boughs and trailing pine ropes to decorate the house. I concentrate on rabbit, squirrel and even deer tracks. This means I often want to go in one direction and she is aimed in another. A tug-of-war can go on between us until I either find a rabbit hole near some evergreens or she decides to set aside her quest to follow me along the animal tracks. Since I am only 15 inches high I am limited on how deep into the snow pack I can maneuver. Jumping through a two foot snow bank can be exhausting. I've been known to disappear on occasion. Imagine yourself under a 10 foot snow pile trying to move, and you'll get the picture.

Once Mom called and called, knowing I must be just ahead of her, but she couldn't see me. Panic set in as she thrashed around in the snow drifts. Then she saw a pair of black pointed ears twitching and heard a muffled bark. "Well, that's either a black eared bunny or my Fergus!" she exclaimed. Digging me out took half an hour and her mittens were soaked. But we were eventually reunited in a cloud of crystal hugs.

To this day they tease me by calling me their "black bunny." This is the ultimate insult for a dedicated rabbit hunter like me. I've been known to go in the hall closet and chew on Dad's bunny hat in response to this insult.

An Angel Gets a Bath

I find Christmas the most exciting holiday
on Lone Pine Road. Dad has "time off" and is
eager to fill it with as many projects as possible.
These projects, in Mom's opinion, rarely have
anything to do with Christmas, or relaxing, or
family. Often Dad says he is working on gifts,
but this is a ploy. Mom does not need a "new"
old clock for Christmas. She does not want the
roof suddenly repaired. She would rather not
think about a new septic tank cover to replace the
cracked one buried under her herb garden. And
taking apart the hot water heater is the last gift
she would ask for. However, Dad has, over the
years, supplied all of these "presents" to Mom.

Mom, for her part, loves everything that
Christmas represents—family, food, and
decorations. She thinks that the "real" reason for
the holiday is all but lost on most humans. Mom
remembers, though. She has been working on a

clay crèche for years. She is more spiritual than religious, so her crèche takes the form of a shack made out of an old wooden crate, featuring (clay) third world people surviving on beans. (Mom's crèche includes real beans.)

Mom has made so many angels that they crowd our house for the month of December and well beyond. Of course, all of Mom's angels are a little quirky. She makes some of them out of old newspaper circulars that advertise all manner of commercial gifts for people to buy. She cuts faces from the ads, little models, which look quizzical, peering out from their paste paper wings. And sometimes she glues on eerily familiar faces, from old photos. She wants to make a statement about how Christmas has become too commercialized.

One year Mom decided to make herself a "Grandmother Angel." She was born after all her grandparents had died, and this had left her with an empty feeling inside. So this angel was to be life-size. Mom began with an armature made of a broom handle, stuck in a heavy pipe with a flange bottom. (You might wonder why, but because of the creation's height, it needed to be sturdy.) Mom covered the broom handle with chicken wire to form a wide skirt, upper torso, and generous arms. And she covered the armature with old damask tablecloths and doilies that her grandmother had made long ago. She formed the angel's head out of plaster and covered it with yarn-hair and more doilies and a halo of gold wire. She fashioned wings from wire clothes hangers, which she covered with tatted-edged hankies, also handed down from some elusive ancestor. To give her "Grandmother" an ethereal presence, Mom lit up her angel from the inside with a small table lamp.

I know all this because Mom has tried to explain the construction of her creation to so many people. (People visiting at Christmas are taken aback upon entering our house to find a human-sized mummy in the corner of the living room where they might have expected to find a tree.) In fact, I know that she was once scared herself half to death by her angel shortly after she set it up. She had come down the stairs for a midnight snack, and bumped into it as she rounded a corner. She screamed bloody murder (which gave me a fright) until she recognized the figure as her self-made grandmother. It was then I took a distinct dislike to this unholy angel.

Mom may find her benign and comforting, but she looks sinister and overpowering to me. Visiting family dogs must agree with me. We often sneak into the living room and take turns "marking" the angel, if you know what I mean. Mom usually discovers this marking long after the deed has been done. With a human's limited sense of smell, she cannot detect the presence of several dog scents. She only knows that a canine has left its mark.

She tends to blame Pepper, Laura's demented dog. Mom does give me a questioning look, too, though. However, since she has read that you must not scold a dog for an infraction unless you actually see him commit one, so I am usually off the hook. But because of this insult, as she sees it (or to be more accurate, smells it), Mom has to give this angel a bath each year. She loosens the angel's tablecloths and soaks them in bluing. She can't fully remove them because they're all sewn to each other and the wire frame at the waistline. While this cleansing takes place, the angel's head flops over from its weight, making her look cross, and her wings droop. I enjoy seeing the angel in this vulnerable position.

Before Mom covers her angel in plastic and stores her in the basement until the following Christmas, she spreads the "skirts" out to dry. So I try to get at least one more "shot" at her. Mom is watchful of her angel after we dogs have besmirched it so often. However, when Dad is working downstairs, I slip by him and give it a little squirt for old time's sake.

Holiday Food Follies

What would the holidays be without food? Mom and I agree they wouldn't be much. In fact our whole extended family (and I bet most of your families) know that food is the secret ingredient which brings everyone together. This doesn't take anything away from religious persuasions. Christians have the Last Supper. Jewish people have Passover. Muslims and Hindus have their feasts, too. It's just that humans and canines have a collective memory of our years during the ice age when roasting mastodon or sizzling boar presented occasions for celebration, in and of themselves. And, once the earth warmed, feasts followed famine. All who survived the famine were grateful for the grain, game and succulent birds that again flourished in their lands. I would hazard a guess that the main reason humans and many other animals spread out across the continents so many eons ago was their search for new nutritional resources, in other words – food.

The discussions in our family about what dishes will find their way to the holiday table start as early as the previous year's repast. Not only that, each holiday meal involves long lingering conversations about all the past holiday meals and their most memorable aspects. Not all of these reminiscences are of perfectly prepared roasts or delectable desserts, however. Our family has had its share of less than successful chefs. As the family "taste tester," I have witnessed a few bad meals myself, but I usually find some edible remains to enjoy. I do get a kick out of hearing how some feckless individual may have completely missed the mark while trying to entertain others over the holidays.

Dad is one of the favorite targets for these culinary critiques. Let's just say that he is not ready to don the chef's cap at even the local fast food joint. Canned baked beans and

Hamburger Helper are two of his mainstays when Mom is away. Even so, he will decide once in a while to entertain others with his culinary skills. The problem is that Dad just doesn't have any culinary skills. Even I have trouble eating what is left behind after Dad has incinerated it on the grill, or "nuked" it in the microwave. Yes – Dad loves microwave ovens.

Mom loves to tell about the time Dad decided he would make Christmas dinner in his brand new microwave oven for her and a few friends. He had a microwave recipe for glazed Cornish hens with rice stuffing. It looked like a fairly simple but elegant dish in the sample photo provided. (Never trust a photo. It was probably a plastic bird slathered with polyurethane in the photo.) Now, whereas Mom might use a microwave to heat water for tea or reheat leftovers, Dad latched onto this handy appliance as a gourmet's greatest friend. To this day he would be totally lost without one in the kitchen.

He has even developed a new form of cooking, which the family has affectionately termed "ralphing." They will say, "He ralphed it," when Mom describes an event where Dad had instantly evaporated a cup of coffee or laminated the inside of the microwave oven with spaghetti sauce.

Dad is a heat transfer expert in his professional life, which makes all this over heating of food more interesting. He likes to find the outside limits of the heating process. He has even used a microwave oven in his class at Penn State to demonstrate how an egg will explode if it is super heated in its shell.

One time, when grandchild Josiah was visiting, Dad set the microwave on fire with over-popped popcorn. He had set the timer for way too long and gone into his den. Smoke alarms went off and flames shot out in a fine display of "over ralphing" or nuking the popcorn. I was there and ran out of the house with Josiah. Mom was gone at the time, so, after putting out the fire, Dad swore Josiah to secrecy. Well it didn't take a heat transfer expert to detect the scent of burnt popcorn. Dad had to replace the appliance and promise Mom never to "ralph" anything again. Good luck.

But this dinner for holiday guests took place way back when Dad was first discovering the microwave's potential. He and Mom were not married yet, and his house was undergoing its extended renovations. The new microwave was the first one this old house had ever had to accommodate. So Dad did some fancy electrical work to fit it just above the conventional stove. He was proud of his work and felt compelled to try it out – cooking a complete meal. Too bad he didn't try it out alone, first, as his unsuspecting guests would learn.

On that auspicious day Mom arrived early to set the table and help out in the kitchen. She was a little concerned about the meal, too.

Two older ladies were invited, and one was Jewish. Sarah was like a mother to Mom. They celebrated most holidays together and Christmas was no exception. Sarah was as open-minded as they come, but Mom didn't want any oddities in the meal to put her off. As Mom chopped the vegetables, she asked some pointed questions about the main course. Dad's anemic-looking Cornish hens were in a baking dish on the counter. "Why haven't you started cooking these birds yet?" Mom asked, "The guests will be here in half an hour."

"Oh it will take no time at all to cook them in the microwave," was Dad's cool reply.

"Well remember that Sarah always has her meat well done. Besides any fowl needs to be thoroughly cooked to avoid giving someone salmonella food poisoning," Mom stated emphatically. She knew these hens would be tenderly roasting in their juices in a regular oven by now if she were in charge. She has never even considered microwaving a hen.

Under pressure Dad proceeded to prepare his main course. He had made cooked rice, celery and mushroom stuffing which he packed into the little birds as if they could expand like balloons. Mom suggested he put some of the stuffing aside before the birds burst their skins. This caused Dad to pout, but he did decide to save a little for the serving platter.

Because the microwaves don't actually brown meat like regular ovens, a glaze becomes necessary to give the meat a "healthy glow." Dad mixed his glaze as the recipe instructed, and put the birds in the oven for ten minutes, as (he thought) the recipe instructed. Mom could not imagine how those hens could possibly be done in that amount of time. However, she had never tried this kind of cooking in a microwave, so she just shrugged her shoulders and went off to set the table.

When Sarah and her friend Molly arrived, Dad was ready with cheese and crackers. He uncorked some good wine (according to Mom, Dad is surprising well versed in the qualities of wine.). All was going swimmingly (Mom's choice of adverb, not mine) when Mom heard the microwave's distinctive "ding."

"I guess it's time to check on the entrée," she said as she stood up.

"Oh no you don't." chimed in Dad. "I'm in charge of this meal," he added with a puffed out chest, looking like a proud peacock, "I'll call you all to the table when the entrée is ready." With that he marched off to the kitchen like a general ready to inspect his troops.

"How lovely that we are getting such special treatment," Sarah cooed.

It was no secret that she absolutely adored Dad. She, Mom and Dad had all met each other on the same day at a singles event. "I'll dance at his wedding," she had said to Mom shortly afterward. So Sarah had followed the budding relationship of these two "youngsters" (Sarah thought anyone under fifty was a youngster.) with great interest. In fact it was she who would encourage them to finally get married and "get it over with." Ralph (Dad) could do no wrong in Sarah's eyes.

When they were summoned, the ladies were delighted with the festive table. There were crystal wine glasses, tall candles and Mom's borrowed silver. Music helped to set the mood. Dad brought in a large platter with honey glazed Cornish hens on a bed of rice stuffing. It looked so fantastic that even Mom was impressed. Each person received a bird of their own.

"Please start while I get the rest, I don't want your hens to get cold," Dad urged. Then he returned to the kitchen to cook the vegetables, which had to wait to be cooked until the microwave was free. Getting all the food to the table at one time was a trick he hadn't yet learned.

Meanwhile, Sarah cut into her bird and took a bite. She got a funny look on her face, which Mom noticed immediately.

"Is something wrong?" Mom asked.

"Oh no," Sarah replied, but she didn't seem to be chewing what was in her mouth. Mom noticed that she looked a little "green around the gills," as humans put it when they see someone about to get sick.

Mom took a bite of her own hen. It wasn't even rare in the middle, it was raw. Oh Lord thought, Mom, we're going to give salmonella to an octogenarian!

She quickly took up a collection of the birds from the table and returned them to the kitchen.

"Ralph, these hens are more ready to fly away than be eaten. They aren't cooked!" she hissed as she went through the swinging door.

"Good Lord. Well let me check the cooking time on my recipe," he sheepishly replied.

It turns out that the recipe was for only one hen. Dad had four hens to cook and didn't realize that with a microwave, cooking time must be multiplied as the amount of food to be cooked increases. (Actually he did know this in theory, but was following his recipe without thinking like an engineer.) The four hens needed about 35 to 40 minutes to be cooked, not the ten minutes that one hen requires. Are you with me? All this gobble-de-gook is confusing I know. To us canines, a bird is a bird, cooked or uncooked, they're delicious. All that matters I guess is that Dad goofed on the time needed to get the birds cooked to human specifications. Also, Mom knew that she could have cooked the hens in a conventional oven in about the same amount of time.

She threw her hands up in the air. "Let's cook two hens at one time. We can split them," she said, "but be sure they're cooked through this time, okay?"

Dad nodded and returned the hens to the oven. Mom went back through the swinging door and made apologies for the delay. Sarah and Molly were patient souls, according to Mom. They seemed to be enjoying the events as a matter of fact. Sarah offered to go help Dad, but she never owned a microwave in her life. Mom said to let the "heat transfer expert" work it out. The three women picked at their Jello salads and talked about children and grandchildren. Each woman knew that cooking is an art not a science, so their expectations for the meal quickly lowered. With each exclamation from the kitchen they would look anxiously at the swinging door to the kitchen. It was as if there was a baby being delivered by a novice physician.

Dad poked his head around the swinging door a couple times to ask Mom a question or say, "It'll just be a few minutes more. I want to make sure these birds are really cooked." Then he'd grin. Mom noticed sweat beading on his brow and felt sympathy for him, along with a kind of superiority (in terms of cooking). The great Dr. Webb had yet to master cooking 101.

All of a sudden the kitchen came alive – as if the hens had regained their breath and decided to take flight. There was a swooshing sound, then a definite "Bang!" as if the oven door had been unhinged. A splattering sound like buckshot filled the room. Mom bolted for the kitchen. The guests froze in place. As the swinging door opened, they saw rice plastered on the ceiling and counter tops. The deflated Cornish hens were bouncing on the floor. This was Dad's most spectacular "ralphing" ever. The overstuffed birds had finally reached the superheating point and exploded with a flourish.

The ladies, unharmed, seemed somehow pleased to be a part of this auspicious occasion. Also they knew that they no longer had to worry about eating the dinner. Even the five second rule couldn't help Dad. (I would have been more than glad to "clean up the mess" if I had been around.) In the end everyone helped to clean it up. Dad offered to take everyone out to eat, but the ladies deferred. Somehow they had lost their appetites.

This was the first and last time Dad ever tried to make Christmas dinner.

Leslie Comes to Visit

You know how someone comes into your
life just when you need a fresh outlook, a
perceptive friend and sympathetic listener?
That's just how it was for Leslie and me. Leslie
is a human, but she understands canines about as
well as any human on the planet. We are now
great friends, and it all happened as the result of
a fiasco, actually a whole set of fiascos.

Mom and Dad, my human companions,
were planning a trip to some place warm. Mom
was the one who hatched the plan. She was
designing a large art quilt which was to feature
undersea life. How any being could go, much
less live, under the sea is beyond me. However,
Mom knew of quite a few creatures that did just
that. She showed me pictures of these creatures,
and by the look of them, I'm glad I will never
have to go there. It was Mom's idea to get up
close and personal with a coral reef, though, to

photograph them. We Scotties enjoy being on *terra firma*, which I think was named after our patriarch – Terrier Firma. Anyway, I was glad to be left out of the travel plans.

"Just a few days of sun and surf," Mom said emphatically. Dad protested as he thought about leaving his pile of consulting research behind. "You can bask in the sun while I take a snorkeling trip out in the bay," she argued. She had the Florida Keys in mind. I don't know what these "keys" are, but I do know that the winters here in Halfmoon Valley can leave a human wondering if evolution really allows them to exist in this frigid a climate. They evolved on a warm savannah somewhere, and it is to that environment they are always gravitating. So, eventually Dad came around and "warmed" to the idea (pun intended) of a few days in the tropics. He could pack his laptop, a thin black box that, when opened, turned his face a greenish color. In fact, he thought he might enjoy learning to snorkel, too. I tried to picture Dad with his pasty white skin in a 1960's era swimsuit paddling out in the deep blue sea with lap top in hand, but it was too painful an image to contemplate for long.

"Okay, I'll arrange the trip," Dad announced the next day.

Mom gave Dad the name of a lovely resort on an island just off shore of the Little Torch Key. There was a national oceanic sea life refuge nearby. She began to have visions of a relaxed, educational, inspiring and warm break from the bleak Pennsylvania winter.

As Dad got on his computer to search for the best airline ticket prices for their trip, Mom got on the phone to find temporary lodgings for me. I never figured out why they didn't just leave me home when they were gone – with a bag of dog food or, better yet, a few pounds of raw beef bones. I usually stay at the Royal Pet Resort, which is a misnomer. There's not much that's royal or resort-like about it. But at least it's clean and dry, and I can go out through a door whenever I want to get fresh air. Well, it turned out that The Royal Pet Resort was undergoing a remodeling, and they couldn't take me. Now Mom had a problem. She wants me to be well taken care of when she's away, so most of the local kennels were out. She ended up booking me into a kennel at a distance from home. It was recommended by a respected animal shelter, which uses space there for homeless canines when needed.

As it turned out, neither the vacation Mom and Dad planned, nor the kennel I was booked into would end up meeting anyone's expectations. I don't know who had the worse time, Mom and Dad or *me*.

Dad got his dates mixed up and had scheduled the airline flights, the hotel room and the rental car for the day *before* they actually left – cutting short their vacation by one day. When they arrived at the airport the day after the reservations specified, they found out that all the original reservations had been cancelled, because Mom and Dad had not shown up on the scheduled day. Somehow Dad talked the airline reservationists into letting them on board another plane, but there would be a long delay at the next airport. Their five day trip was now down to four days. After a long wait for a plane to Miami, they were stuck in a seedy hotel waiting to get to Key West. They didn't sleep that night, because there was a huge fight at the hotel's "night club." Police sirens went off periodically as they arrived to establish some semblance of "law and order." With Mom and Dad's room so close to all the action, it must have been scary. And I wasn't there to protect them.

Meanwhile, I was back at the dog kennel with all the homeless dogs. I made out okay on the first day. I had my bed from home and several of my favorite chew toys. I was lonely, though, and disturbed by all the barking that went on day and night. Some of my kennel mates had no human companions. They were without a family to care for them, so their barking was more like a continuous lament.

The second day Mom and Dad finally made it to the resort. However, it wasn't what Mom had expected. Dad had saved money by booking a room at the marina for the resort. The resort was actually off shore and inaccessible to anyone but paying guests. This on shore holding zone had none of the amenities of the main resort. There was no beach and no swimming pool – just a rough coral pad with a dock for boats. This came as a shock to Mom, who was so disappointed she almost cried. I won't repeat what she had to say to Dad about all this. Let's just say that it would have caused a lot of bleeping if she had said it on TV. But at least the little bungalow had a clean bed, and it was quiet way out there off the beaten track. Mom calmed herself with the thought of going out to the living reef on a snorkeling tour the next day.

That night they went out to dinner at a nice seafood restaurant. The atmosphere was festive and relaxing. Mom began to feel as if they were now on vacation. All went beautifully until their waitress, while bringing their order, suddenly got sick and had to rush to the ladies room holding her hand over her mouth. She was gone for good. Needless to say, they didn't eat what she had served. The manager apologized and offered a gift card for the next night. They stopped to get a couple fast food burgers, and headed back to their tiny "piece of paradise" feeling tired and dejected.

On the way back Dad suggested a little walk around the compound to cheer them up. They pulled up to their less than elegant accommodations, and Dad went inside. He came out, shut the door behind him and took Mom's arm. They tried to see their way around in the dark, but the marina was poorly lighted. It wasn't a good idea to stumble around for long in the dock area, so they returned to their room, eager to get some quality sleep.

"What a day," said Mom, thinking of how stressful it had been.

"Tomorrow will be better," said Dad in a hopeful tone.

When they returned to their room they found the door locked.

"Get out the key," mumbled Mom already in slumber mode.

"Oh God, I locked it in the room," came the shaky reply.

Mom was not amused. "How could you do that?"

Dad had left both the room key and the rental car keys on the table when he went in to the bathroom. He didn't realize the outside doors would automatically lock behind him. It was 10:30 p.m. now, the marina, where the master keys were kept was locked. No one was around. In a panic Dad decided to look for help. Not a soul was there, but he did find the little dive shop next door unlocked. He slipped in and used the phone to call the sheriff.

"We don't come out to do that kind of work," he was told. "Get a locksmith." This was not a sympathetic sheriff. Mom couldn't believe the sheriff wouldn't come to help them.

By now it was 11p.m. and there wasn't even a reclining patio chair to sleep on. They couldn't go somewhere else to find a room because the car was locked up tight. Dad riffled through some drawers in the dive shop, found a few screw drivers, and returned to their room. Mom was sort of sobbing quietly while propped against the French doors leading to a cozy bed and much needed bathroom. Dad gently moved Mom aside by the shoulders and inspected the doors. "Aha," he said. "The hinges are on the outside. Any fool could get these doors off."

"I sure hope that includes you," was Mom's cryptic reply.

Soon Dad was undoing the bolts. Mom now hoped that the sheriff was as lazy as he sounded, because they were "breaking and entering" for sure. The plan was for Mom to hold up the two heavy interlocked glass doors while Dad wiggled his way inside to unlock them. He got the hinges off fairly rapidly then pushed an opening between the doors and the frame. When he did this, they began to tilt and almost came crashing down on Mom. As they fell out toward her, she spread her legs wide, stiffened her outspread arms, and used all the reserve energy she had to push the doors back toward Dad. She was splayed across the doors like a giant arachnid (spider). And she could have been squashed like a bug had the doors tilted much farther and reached their tipping point.

Dad was inside. He grabbed the door knobs just in time. He used all his strength to keep the doors from squashing Mom. He unlocked them and put them back on the hinges. It was after 12 a.m. when they collapsed into bed.

Back at the kennel I was miserable. It started to rain in the morning. It rained and rained and rained. There was no solid door between the inside and outside of my cubicle, so the water just seeped in onto the cement floor. I watched as puddles began to gather then collected and pooled inside. My bed was on a little platform, just inches above the concrete floor. It was almost floating. Remember, I am an "earth dog." This turn of events was scary. I was thinking that Mom and Dad had deserted me to have a good time far away, which made me more miserable.

You're wondering by now where Leslie comes into this tale of woe. Well, this is one of those stories that builds on misfortune to make the happy ending that much more satisfying. It's like an O Henry story. Mom and Dad are miserable and I am miserable, but we each think the other is doing fine. Somehow I survived the night where I was, and Mom and Dad got some sleep in Florida. They had to get up very early, though, to catch their scheduled boat to the coral reef area.

I just want to say that Mom was so emotional when she told this next part of the story that I didn't get it all. Suffice it to say the boat was OLD. The "guides' were a motley crew. They managed to lose one propeller going out to the reef and one coming back into the dock.

The boat carried only one spare, and the repair took so long going out that the boat did not even get close to the coral reef. The site where it stopped was too deep for snorkeling, and the water was very choppy. Dad swam out in the wrong direction and Mom had to swim out and get him back. He had heard the boatman mention "man of war" and thought there was a shipwreck to explore. He didn't know this phrase also meant a dangerous kind of jellyfish. People on board were warned to stay away from the very area Dad was trying to explore. By the time Mom caught up with him, people were getting back in the boat. There were no colorful fish or coral reef photographs to bring back from this trip, and the only tangible evidence that Mom had been out of Halfmoon Valley was a sunburn from swimming out to retrieve Dad.

When Mom finally came to pick me up, it was still raining. My bed was soaked and the barking had increased from my fellow "inmates." I was bedraggled and shivering. Mom was so incensed when she saw the terrible conditions at the kennel, she demanded to know how this could have happened. "You people ought to be reported!" she shouted at the owners.

"We just weren't prepared for this kind of rain," the owners replied.

"Well my dog will never again have to endure a place like this," Mom retorted. I'm not sure she even paid them.

I climbed gratefully into our little red van and sniffed around for familiar smells. It had only been four days, but it seemed an eternity since I had been safe and warm – and the little red van was as good as home to me. Mom wrapped me in a warm blanket and promised to find someone special to take care of me at home the next time she and Dad would be away. And she meant it.

The next year at Christmas time, when Mom and Dad were to go to Missouri to see Arleigh and Ellyn dance in the Nutcracker, Mom asked and asked around until she heard about a very special person, who takes care of animals in their own homes. She found Leslie, and so Mom kept her promise. As Christmas approached,

Mom began making preparations as if they weren't going away. She decorated with her usual plethora of "arty" objects, as Dad calls them, and put up the tree with all its quirky ornaments. She baked some cookies and even filled a stocking for Leslie. She left treats for me, too.

At first I was a little standoffish with Leslie. She had come into my domain and set up camp. I wasn't used to strangers, and always suspected they might not understand my preeminence in the household. When Mom and Dad went out, I thought of myself as the security detachment left to guard the property. I took my work very seriously, too. Who was this upstart who seemed to be at home in my house? Well, I learned that she was someone with lots of treats and a warm affectionate personality for starters. Mom was surprised, too, that Leslie brought her own inflatable bed, covers, even food.

Leslie and I became great buddies over time, eating together, walking together, and she even let me sleep on a great big bed that she pumped up at night so we could sleep comfortably on the floor. Christmas with Leslie was full of surprises and extra treats. On Christmas we opened our gifts together. But, the best present of all was that I never had to leave home again, because each time Mom and Dad went away Leslie would come to stay with me.

Where there is Smoke....

Some Christmases many family members gather at Lone Pine and other years only a few assemble. Mom and Dad have combined families that visit in rotating packs of grownups, kids, and pets. Aunt Sandy and Uncle Bruce are usually amongst the visitors to our house ever since they returned from England. Living there, they missed family gatherings, so they make it a point to be part of our holiday events. Uncle Bruce once arrived in a full leg cast. He had broken his hip skating and had to ride with his seat in the car pushed all the way back and his leg propped on the dashboard for the fourteen-hour trip from Maine. To say he is a hardy soul is an understatement. Sandy and Bruce always bring Rosie, so I have extended family to play with when they visit.

We have a large fireplace, which, according to Mom, adds to the holiday atmosphere. I am not particularly fond of fire, though, and for good reason—the size and scope of Dad's fires are frightening. Dad builds indoor bonfires. And he has a whole ritual involved with his fire building. He begins with piles of newspaper that he scrunches into a small mountain. Then he covers the newspaper with enough kindling to burn down a small barn. Lastly, he adds huge logs, small tree trunks actually, left after the property was cleared to build the house. Now too weathered for Mom's precise artwork, the cherry wood fits Dad's needs perfectly. Cherry is a hardwood that burns with tremendous heat once it takes the flame. Dad always surveys his "fire sculpture" to make sure there will be enough oxygen available to get things blazing. Then he readies to light his masterpiece.

Now Dad never forgets his engineering practices. This means that he needs at least one gadget to complete a project. The gadget he has chosen for lighting fires is a propane torch.

That's right, a blowtorch. It is a small one, to be sure, but impressive nonetheless. I usually exit the premises as soon as I see this baby emerge from behind the chimney corner. Using a blowtorch is a sure fire way (pun intended) to get a blaze going. For protection, Dad wears a thick leather, gauntlet-type glove on the hand in which he holds the torch. He leaves the welder's mask in the workshop, although it might be nice if he wore one for safety's sake. To make matters worse, he is known to leave the torch lit and point it into the fire long after the fire has caught. He says that by doing this, he insures that the fire will not fizzle out. This practice is overkill in my estimation. His fires are as close to spontaneous combustion as a human can create; they ignite instantly, giving off incredible heat.

While Dad's fire building alarms Mom, she is usually in the kitchen, and misses most of the ritual. Bruce and Sandy, however, could not believe their eyes when Dad got the blowtorch from its "hiding place." To say they were alarmed the first time they saw it, is an understatement. Aunt Sandy began to shriek, "What the H— are you doing?"

"This always works," replied Dad calmly.

"You're going to burn the house down!"

"Hasn't happened yet," Dad said, becoming a little agitated.

"Well, how about if I build the next fire?" suggested Bruce, trying to avoid any conflict.

"Okay," says Dad, playfully throwing down the gauntlet. Long ago, when knights engaged in combat over the slightest thing, this act was meant as a challenge to a joust. Even earlier, in prehistoric times, making a steady fire was necessary for survival. So Bruce understood that he was challenged to make a better fire. It is part of being macho for human males to demonstrate this skill. But this challenge business often becomes exaggerated.

Now Sandy and Bruce have reason to worry about huge, stoked fires. A few years before they moved to England, their teenage son, Danny, alone on the lower floor of the family home decided to get a real fire going in the wood stove. He kept feeding the flames with small pieces of wood that burned very fast. The heat built up in the chimney to the point that it started a roof fire. Neighbors saw the smoke and flame and called the fire department. Before Danny had any idea he was creating such destruction, fire engines were screaming up the road. The fire fighters barged into the house, ascended to the roof and chopped a few holes in it in order to determine the fire's origin. Thank goodness, they arrived quickly. They saved the house, but it was inconvenient to have a hole in the roof in the middle of winter. Danny later said that he just wanted to keep his feet warm.

Bruce has been cautious around fires ever since that incident occurred. The day after Dad's "barn burner," he approached his fire building "according to the Boy Scout manual." He started the fire with much less paper and kindling than Dad had started with. He chose the best logs for the fire, splitting some of them outdoors so that they would be just the right size. He laid the logs in the fireplace in a lovely radial pattern. His fire building was a work of art. He knew he could light his fire with just one match and that it would burn slowly and evenly for hours. He proudly lit the fire with a flourish. It began to burn with a pleasant glow.

The one thing Bruce forgot to do (and that Dad had neglected to point out to him) was to open the flue to allow smoke to escape up the chimney. In our fireplace, the flue lever is located inside our big hearth, slightly hidden from sight. Dad knew from experience that opening the flue is not an easy thing to do once a fire is already going. Did he forget to tell Bruce about the lever? We have never answered this question. What we do know is that the smoke and ash from Bruce's beautiful fire began escaping into the room. It billowed. It curled. It chased every one of us out of the house to escape its choking fumes. But Dad stayed behind to open the flue and wave the smoke out of the house.

It was freezing outside. Mom had grabbed some blankets on the way out and the humans huddled together beneath them like displaced refugees. I carry a warm coat with me everywhere I go, so I just enjoyed an unexpected frolic in the snow. Dad opened all the windows and emerged from the house coughing. Bruce was mortified. But we all began to see the humor in the event by suppertime, when our reliable furnace warmed up the house again.

Dogs do not laugh, but we do roll around in the snow when life seems irresistibly funny.

Dancing with Frosty

When I first came to live at the Lone Pine house, Mom was inexperienced with canine companionship. It took time for her to relax around me. She seemed like the typical uptight female. Finding a balance between us was going to take patience on both our parts. So I was open to any signs that she could unwind in my presence. Eventually I could tell my influence on her was real. She went from being an overbearing "dog handler" to being a true companion. We began to form a bond that was truly reciprocal over dancing – that's right dancing. It all happened like this.

As I observed Mom in the studio one day I made the discovery that although she could not sing well, (in fact causing me ear pain if I was anywhere nearby) she liked to dance to loosen up for her artwork. She moved like a clumsy, but happy, puppy. Whenever she worked in the studio, she put on music, and her favorite was classical jazz. She would put paint on the canvas with rapid strokes to the music of Duke Ellington or Miles Davis (I learned their names later.). This music seemed to free her up and add life to her artwork. At the time she had no idea anyone was watching. I didn't count as anyone yet. To her I was still just a dog.

Once in a while she let herself go and whirled around the studio like a soul possessed. I loved to see her behave so freely and wanted to encourage it. So one day I hopped out of my comfortable bed and danced around the large studio with her. *Then I got noticed.* The first time I got up on my hind legs to imitate the human form, Mom nearly fell over. I'm a very dignified canine, and this spontaneous behavior surprised even me. What was I doing? I sure hoped there were no wild creatures looking in the windows. We were on ground level and open to the woods.

Mom took hold of my front paws for a few moments and we did the quick step or some such dance together. She laughed and almost knocked over her easel in the excitement. It was the beginning of our companionship and the end of "dog handling" as she realized I was not just a dumb animal, but a being with a personality all my own. We only danced together a few times. The moments of unselfconscious frivolity were rare – and more than a little embarrassing for me. However, they helped us forge a bond that said, "I trust you enough to be completely silly in your presence."

It was shortly after one of these dancing sessions that Mom sat down on the floor with me and recalled the story of an embarrassing incident from her own childhood. Now she didn't need to retell the story in human words. We canines are so attune to our human companions that they only have to relive the event in their minds for us to understand what occurred. We piece it all together from eye movements and body language.

This particular event took place when Mom was in second grade. The holidays were approaching and a Christmas pageant with music, dance and reciting was being planned for the whole school and the parents, too. (That was back when holidays were still called by their original names in school.) Other students were talking about playing instruments, reciting poetry and singing. One girl even had a ballerina costume and had a practiced routine to dance. Mom (whose nickname was Sibby) wanted to be a part of the pageant too, but she wasn't sure how she might perform. It seemed like everyone had a talent except for her. She and her sister had been put in the back row of the children's choir at church and told to try and listen more than sing. So she realized singing solo at the pageant was out of the question.

Then one day Sibby's dad brought home a Gene Autry record (He was one of those singing cowboys.) on which was the song "Frosty the Snowman." Well, Sibby had never heard the song before but fell instantly in love with it. The more she played it the happier she became. Now this was before all the TV shows which featured the song, so it was new to everyone else too. Sibby sang the song out loud and in her head over and over. The part about dancing all over town gave her courage.

"I'm going to dance to 'Frosty the Snowman' for my class," she declared to her family at dinner one night, after listening to the recording and secretly trying out her steps. She didn't see all the eyes rolling. Soon she was ready to work out her costume. A flouncey white dress with a big crinoline slip was appropriated from her mother's closet. It was one she and her sister had "trimmed" to size one day when playing circus. She found an old top hat of her father's covered in dust in the back of his closet. (It seems that her parents were not getting out as much since the children had arrived.) She placed it on her head and began to dance around. The cane was in the hall stand just waiting for her. (Little did she know that her father would have a severe stroke and need that cane in just two years.) She had a pair of Mary Jane shoes that could almost make the sound of tap shoes.

Sibby practiced and practiced mimicking the moves she had seen Fred Astair and Ginger Rogers do in the old movies on television. Tap dance is easy she thought. You just slap your feet on the floor a lot. All auditions for the school pageant began in the classroom. Solo participants were to be chosen by their fellow classmates, so that each classroom would be represented. Mom was naïve at the time (actually, she still is). She was confident on the day of her performance that she would "wow" her classmates with her new found talent. The fact that her family had been less than enthusiastic during her "dress rehearsal" at home had not shaken her too much. She was used to getting razzed by her siblings.

After the Suzuki violinist, who broke a string in the middle of his performance, the ballet dancer, who was a little shaky, and a singer who was off key, Sibby thought she had a real chance to be in the pageant. She placed her props – hat and cane – on the big table in front of the class and jumped up on the table. Her crinoline slip caught on the edge of the table and tore so that it was hanging down in the back. She didn't notice until she heard a few twitters from the audience. No time to change, though, she thought, the show must go on. The table wobbled a little. She steadied herself and cued the teacher to start the music. Frosty the Snowman filled the room and her feet began to move. The table continued to wobble noticeably as she slapped her heels against its uncertain surface. Because of this shaky table, she began to have her first ever attack of motion sickness. She must have looked more like a drunken sailor on shore leave than a dapper snowman. The giggles were even coming from her friends now. Only the teacher smiled encouragingly. But did she have a look of embarrassment for her student?

When the music stopped Sibby knew that her dream of a career as a Radio City Rockette was on the rocks. She ended up in the pageant's chorus line as a Christmas tree wearing a green crepe paper dress and brown knee socks. Trees don't dance. A chubby classmate, dressed like a snowball did a stupid dance around her to the tune of "Oh Christmas Tree."

Imagining Mom as a clumsy little girl was amusing but also a little heart breaking. Although she didn't have rhythm, at least she found the courage to let loose once in a while. My muscles didn't allow me to get up on my hind legs for too many years. But music, especially jazz, still makes me tap my paws as I remember our dancing duets and Mom's early attempt at stardom.

The Little House on the Prairie

Christmas always seemed to make Dad a little nostalgic. Normally a very analytic type, he had a strong sentimental streak regarding domestic life. So the movies which Mom loved about people reuniting at the holidays often made Dad cry. That's right, cry. The first time I witnessed this phenomenon I was so shocked I had to climb on his lap to make sure they were real tears. Mom might get misty eyed watching a "chick flick", but to see this often abrupt, sometimes grumpy individual weep over a fictional story always amazed me. Where did this response come from?

Gradually I began to understand this "soft spot" better as I observed him around the house. The saying, "His home is his castle," fit Dad perfectly. The way he cared for our house revealed a strong affection for the very timbers that held it up. He was the one who polished the fixtures and fixed the porch railings, door jams, and loose floor boards with a dedication that made whatever he fixed better than new. He may have been clumsy with mechanical devices, but he always kept at a project until he got it right – even if in doing so he drove Mom to distraction. I once saw him completely disassemble a clock to clean it, then reassemble it, taking a great deal more time, as he had forgotten what parts went where.

One day I was given a real insight into Dad's home loving trait. He had ordered a shed to be made for our Lone Pine property. It was meant to keep all the extra tools and riding mower (and, of course, it is the shed in which I got locked, as told in my memoirs). A crew of Amish workmen arrived with this little building on top of a giant flatbed truck. Dad and the men worked on a gravel pad for its foundation. Then they carefully lowered the building into place. Mom watched the proceedings with a gleam in her eyes. She was tickled that the shed was the same color as the big house. It had two little windows in front with shutters that also matched our house. She was so pleased she clapped her hands like a little girl. "This is a miniature of our home!" she declared. She had never had a playhouse as a girl, so this was a charming, if belated, substitute to decorate – at least the outside. She envisioned window boxes and little curtains.

Dad was more sober, but seemed equally touched by its likeness to the big house. Did I see a tear or two drop from his cheeks? The next day after putting some plants around the shed and installing the tools, he took Mom by the arm, leading her out to see his handywork. (I was busy at the time sniffing around the shed to find out if chipmunks had taken up residence underneath it at the time.)

"Sylvia," he said, "this little shed is 18 feet by 8 feet, and it's exactly the same size as the house my whole family lived in during the depression in the 1930's."

Mom had been aware that Dad's family had been very poor in the wake of the Great Depression. However, since she hadn't been born yet (She's 10 years younger than Dad.), her understanding of the struggle to survive in Kansas at that time was limited. She looked at the shed, then at the big house we live in, then at Dad. She realized that the big house could hold six or seven sheds of this size inside its walls. "Oh Ralph," was all she said, but Dad knew she now had some idea of what his life was like during the dust bowl years out on the plains. Mom had known poverty, but had never lived in anything this small.

Of course, I like small dwellings. My ancestors the wolves knew a cozy place when they found one. They also invented "heat by convection" as Dad calls it. The whole pack huddles together sharing their body heat to keep warm. Our big Lone Pine house is altogether too big for my taste, so I tried to imagine Mom, Dad and I snuggled together in the shed. It was then that I tapped into Dad's memories as he stood there looking at the new little building. We did some time traveling back to when he was a little boy back on the prairie.

It was Christmas time and he was five years old. This was the end of a very difficult year for his family. His father had only earned $64 for the whole previous year. The "Dust Bowl" was reoccurring dry storms of swirling clouds that lifted the loose soil off the flat land and wiped out crops as it tore through the plains states for years. Because of these problems little Ralph's dad left his farm and family behind to look for work in the oil fields of Illinois. His mother was left with two little boys to survive on what little food they could grow. It was a pretty bleak time, but Ralph was young and happy, especially when he visited his grandparents' farm down the road. Granddad Webb was a jolly man who managed to smile despite the harsh conditions he faced everyday.

As the Christmas of 1939 approached, Ralph knew Santa would come. He said over and over, "I can feel it in my bones," mimicking his Grandfather's deep baritone. His mother tried to make the house festive, with pictures cut from an old magazine and pine boughs from the woods, but her heart wasn't in it. The boys were not encouraged to dream of Santa or to see their father any time soon. There was a big wood stove in the living room to keep them warm and home canned food to keep them going.

In the Kansas twilight on Christmas Eve, Ralph, his brother John and his mom gathered around the stove and told stories. Ralph especially liked stories about animals, like those of Beatrix Potter. He identified with Peter Rabbit. (That must be when his fascination with bunnies started.) When it was time for bed Ralph asked his mother, "When do you think Santa will come?"

His mother just shook her head. She didn't want to encourage this fantasy. But just as the boys were headed upstairs, Ralph heard a noise outside. He ran down to the front door. A buggy had pulled up to the house. Ralph saw a large figure in a red suit climb out and unload a heavy object.

"Santa," Ralph cried, "Santa did come!"

"Ho Ho Ho," said Santa as he swung open the door. "I want you all to have a good Christmas." The heavy object he carried turned out to be a bushel basket full of presents for the whole family.

Something about the way Santa walked and his voice made little Ralph think of his grandfather. Of course, he thought, Santa is an old guy too. But there was so much excitement he didn't dwell on the similarity. He was transfixed with joy, as only a five-year-old can be. They toys looked a little familiar, too. But the ones he had were broken and rusty. The ones Santa brought were shiny and looked like new. It was many years later that Ralph learned that his grandfather had collected the broken toys and fixed them like new, giving each a fresh coat of paint.

Soon after the New Year another miracle occurred. Ralph's father came home with a huge truck, owned by the oil company he worked for. On the back of the truck was a tiny house. (You guessed it – 8 by 18 feet). He was treated to shouts of joy from the boys and a home cooked meal from his wife. Days later, the family packed their belongings and traveled from oil field to oil field, whenever his father would be working on a new well. Each time they moved, the little house was carefully carried on the back of the company truck then lowered on to a gravel pad.

Living in this little house was heaven for a small boy, despite the fact that there was no running water, and he had to go outside to an outhouse for "his business." Cooking was done on the top of a wood stove which provided heat in the winter. The family ate at a table on one end of their home. The table was also used for homework, reading, games and family prayers. It was like camping everyday. But most of all, Ralph loved it because his whole family was together everyday. Ralph could smell his father's pipe tobacco and touch his tools (even though he wasn't supposed to) knowing that he would he home for dinner. This is also when Ralph began a lifelong habit of picking things up off the ground. He discovered all manner of machine parts, broken tools and shiny metal objects discarded by the oil field workers. These treasures were collected and often repaired by this budding engineer.

The third miracle arrived less than a year later. His parents came home to the little house one day with a baby wrapped in a pink blanket. Ralph and John now had a baby sister to play with – as soon as she could walk. The baby slept in a tiny crib next to his parent's big bed. When the boys' bed was unrolled at night, the family took up most of the space in the little house. They lived this way, going from oil field to oil field for several years before returning to their farm in Kansas. Ralph's father had provided for the family and saved his farm without ever taking a cent from the government. He was very proud of that achievement.

I can see why Dad (Ralph) loved this kind of living. It must have been a cozy den-like dwelling, not unlike the dens my wolf relatives still build. And I wished for a few moments that I could have joined him back then. The smells of cooking, body heat, pipe tobacco and baby's breath would have been intoxicating for me.

Dad and I snapped out of our reverie to see Mom marking a path from the big house to the little one. "I'll plant flowers along here this spring," she said, "but I'm sure glad we don't have to live in such a little house." Dad and I were not quite so sure.

The Night the Animals Talked

Christmas Eve in Halfmoon Valley presents cold realities and magical promises all wrapped up with stars. Mom and I were out for our evening walk, but this time we were going beyond our usual turn around spot at the end of Lone Pine Road. We turned left onto Sawmill Road and started up the hill toward the Barr Farm. It was a crisp night and the stars gleamed like the eyes of my ancestors, the wolves. There was no snow but I could smell it coming, maybe tomorrow, I thought. I listened for the nocturnal movements in the hedges and windrows which framed Sawmill Road.

I knew there were lots of nocturnal animals going about their lives in the wildwoods and fields surrounding us. While humans make the most noise and take up the most space with their houses and cars, they aren't the most numerous animals in Halfmoon Valley. As a

121

dog, I'm aware of both humans and all these other animals. We dogs are "mediums" between the humans and other animals – their connecting links. This means I know just how crowded a place our valley is. There are more cows than people, and we were headed toward Barr Farm where a number of them resided. Some humans come out here from the towns and say how quiet it is. However, they would hear all kinds of animals and insects if they listened. They would hear the creaking of the tree branches as squirrels bound along them, the scattering sounds of furry mice and voles searching for food, the yawn of the bear, and, yes, the farts of the cows, if they cared to listen intently, but most don't. (As for smells, don't get me started. Humans have lost most of their capacity for scent.) Mom, however, is more sensitive to nature than most humans. Perhaps it's because she's an artist, or perhaps she's an artist because she's more sensitive. In fact, I think I have played a role in helping her to become even more aware of the sights, sounds and even scents out in the wild. The world is active and crowded with life out here, even on a cold winter night. Mom's not scared or worried, though, because she knows she has me to protect and guide her.

As we walked on this particular night, Mom began to relate a story from her childhood that helps to explain why she's so aware of her fellow creatures. It's a Christmas story and would reveal why we were going toward the Barr Farm. When she was young she lived in an old farm house, which her father was in the process of restoring and expanding for his growing family. He was a traveling salesman, so the work went slowly. The family had lived in the city until Sylvia (Mom) and her twin sister, Sandy, turned five years old. Living in the country was a huge change for everyone. Even though Mom (Sibby being her nickname, we'll use it here) and her twin sister slept together each night, they usually went their separate ways during the day. Sandy was in search of other children to play with, while Sibby was more interested in exploring her new surroundings alone.

Sibby's favorite book was Wind in the Willows, about a mole, a rat and a toad of all creatures! I can't even imagine how anyone could grow fond of these vermin, but Mom, oops, Sibby, did. She wondered if creatures like these were to be found in the woods and fields near her new (old) home. She found a tiny stream not far away and sat for hours, hoping to see Mole or Rat emerge from the undergrowth.

Sadly their world seemed invisible to her. And the toads she saw would never have driven a motor car like Toad of Toad Hall. But she was happy to be outdoors, absorbing the sights and sounds around her. I just wish she had had a dog like me to join her as she walked the fields and sat by the stream as a child. (I

would have sniffed out those critters for her.)
Her father had hunting dogs, but they were kept
in a kennel behind the house.

When Sibby was seven years old, her
father brought home a wild baby rabbit in a
basket. He had found it on the roadside while
coming back from one of his long trips. Oscar,
the name they gave it, didn't live very long –
wild bunnies need their mothers – but he had
awakened Sibby's heart to the abundant nature of
life in the wild. She was reading on her own
now and got a book out of the library about a
chipmunk caught in a hunter's coffee pot. It
escaped, but just. "Poor chipmunk," she
thought, "caught in what must have felt like a
terrible trap." (When she told me this part of the
story, I felt a tinge of guilt for chasing
chipmunks.) Her father was a hunter, so when
he brought home a deer he had shot, she cried in
dismay, "You may have killed Bambi's mother!"

Sibby was eight years old or so when television first came into her life. The little black screen produced moving pictures at certain times of the day. The black box seemed like pure magic. It took her eyes a while to adjust to the constant activity on the screen. Through it she was experiencing many strange wonders from far beyond her country home. There were dancers, singers, comics, and stiff men talking in front of maps. There were stories of people in distress and people in love. She began to understand that the Wide World was filled with humans of all kinds – heroes and villains, wise men and fools. Her interest in the world just outside her door faded. Watching television often replaced her walks out in the wildwood.

However a few television shows appeared which reawakened her interest in nature. One was *Zoo America*, which featured all kinds of wild animals from all over the world. Another was *Lassie Come Home*, which entranced her. Lassie was a dog with the empathy, intelligence and grace of a truly great being. This canine continually rescued his "master" from peril. The show emphasized the important role of this animal in human lives. (Lassie, of course, was not unlike many canines through our long association with humans. We tend to think humans are smarter than us, but they are constantly getting in trouble and need an intelligent dog to get them out of trouble.)

Sibby watched and absorbed the idea that humans and animals are not so different one from the other. She decided to resume her walks outdoors and began sketching what she saw. Her mother had enrolled her and her sister in art school. Her teacher, Walter Baum, encouraged her to take her paints outside and try to capture what she experienced there.

By the age of nine, Sibby realized that television was no longer as compelling as it had been. There remained several television shows that she watched religiously, though. One was *Father Knows Best*, which comforted her when her father was away on his long trips. Another was *Leave It to Beaver*, a comic look at growing up in America. Her favorite show of all was *I Remember Mama*. The mama in *I Remember Mama* was a tall soft spoken matronly woman with the kindest eyes Sibby had ever seen. Mama had an accent which could have been Scandinavian and she was raising lots of children in a farm house like the one in which Sibby and her family lived. Since Sibby's own mother was often "sick in bed," the Mama on television became a kind of surrogate mother. She was wise and full of humor at the same time. Her offspring got in all kinds of trouble, but she always handled situations with a calm loving approach. Here was the perfect role model – the one who really "knew best."

One episode of *I Remember Mama* settled into Sibby's consciousness and stays with her even now.

Now we had come to the central part of her story. I love this story best of all because it's mainly about animals. Mama and her family (on television) had animals in the barn next to their house. These animals were part and parcel of the life of the family. Cows had to be milked, chickens fed and eggs collected. There was also a donkey which served some unexplained tasks.

This bygone family (early 20th century), as I said, lived in a place not unlike the place where Sibby's family now lived – with the same kinds of animals nearby. It was Christmas Eve in the story, and, as she did the dishes with her girls helping, Mama told them that in her home country there was a legend that on Christmas Eve, just as the clock struck midnight, all the animals could talk, but only for a few moments. Because Jesus was born in a stable and the animals witnessed his birth, they were allowed to proclaim the event each year. Most of Mama's children, being "sophisticated Americans," found this story highly unlikely. But the youngest, Dagmar, whose character was about Sibby's age at the time, was captivated by the idea. She decided to stay up and find out if the legend was true. Dagmar sneaked down stairs and lit a candle, then went out to the barn. Mom is unclear what happened next, but she remembers the animals in the stable (in the story) were talking. These were real animals, not the animal puppets on *Mr. Rogers' Neighbor* or Howdy Dowdy, or cartoon characters, which seemed to make fun of animals. No. There was a real cow mooing one moment, then saying to a donkey, "A child is born who will change the world!" Sibby was transfixed. The girl Dagmar had fallen asleep in the hay.

Memory is a funny thing. What was real and what one wishes were real may get confused in our minds. But somehow the little girl nicknamed Sibby, who became an artist and a mother, and my human companion, heard the animals talk on Christmas Eve. She knew it was only a television show, but there was a truth revealed to her that night – animals have abilities we often ignore or overlook. They are sentient beings and deserve to be treated with respect. That is why most of Mom's artwork centers on the natural world. For her there is magic in the rocks and trees and the most humble flowers, and animals are out there managing to survive in a world we can only imagine.

Back in real time, Mom and I walked up the hill toward the shack where the donkeys live. These creatures have such soulful faces it's easy to imagine them witnessing a momentous event, like the first Christmas, and passing on the knowledge of it to succeeding generations. The cows right across the road didn't seem interested in us or the donkeys, but they were mooing in a strange way that night. Perhaps they were speaking in a different human language from English. (As we canines know, animals talk to each other in their own languages all the time.)

In the *I Remember Mama* story, the animals waited until the children had gone to sleep to speak. Mom doesn't remember all the details anymore, but she wanted to come up to where these animals lived this special night "to pay her respects" she said. But, from the childlike look on her face, I suspected she was reliving a childhood fantasy of waiting for the animals to speak in her language. We turned around after a few minutes, and I think Mom wondered if the animals would have a conversation after she left. As for me, the walk was worth it just to see Mom's face as she remembered "Mama" and the legend of the animals.

Not too long ago Mom made a quilt titled "Amish Nativity." In the center design Mom painted the holy family in a stable, dressed in Amish clothes. There are all kinds of animals surrounding the baby Jesus. And I know now why the donkey and cows seem so important to the scene. It's because Mom (Sibby) still wonders about the legend of animals talking on Christmas Eve.

Made in the USA
Charleston, SC
15 June 2013